It's exciting to ... I watch it in action as it ... hough, since many s...

To help you identify Southeast and Gulf States shorebirds, this guide covers 72 species, grouping them by feeding activity. Simply observe their feeding behavior while the birds swim, walk or fly, and then turn to the matching thumb tab.

Probing Feeders

Look for:	round-bodied, often long-billed and long-legged birds, scouring and probing shores
Habitat:	beaches, shallow water, ponds, lakes, also marshes, wetlands and mudflats

Wading Feeders

Look for:	long-legged birds, often standing in water before striking at prey
Habitat:	surf, shores, lakes, rivers, ponds, wetlands, bogs, wet ditches, swamps and estuaries

Plunging Feeders (Terns)

Look for:	usually white birds, frequently in flocks, plunging headfirst from flight into water
Habitat:	shores, lakes and marshes

Scavenging Feeders (Gulls)

Look for:	usually larger white birds, often in flight, scavenging on water and land
Habitat:	shores, lakes, rivers, suburban and urban areas

Dabbling Feeders

Look for:	water birds with their heads underwater and their rumps in the air
Habitat:	shallow to deep water, beaches, ponds, rivers, lakes and estuaries

Diving Feeders

Look for:	water birds diving, completely submerging their bodies underwater
Habitat:	deep water, shores, ponds, lakes and rivers

Least Sandpiper
yellow-to-green legs and thin, slightly down-curved bill

non-breeding

Western Sandpiper
down-curved black bill, rufous back

non-breeding

Sanderling
black legs, usually in small groups on beaches

non-breeding

Spotted Sandpiper
spots on chest and belly, pumps tail up and down

non-breeding

SANDPIPERS

6"   6 1/2"   8"   8"

Dunlin
black belly, long
down-curved bill

non-breeding

Solitary Sandpiper
dull olive legs, white spots
on dark wings and back

non-breeding

Pectoral Sandpiper
yellow legs and bill,
large head

Purple Sandpiper
overall dark, short bill

SANDPIPERS

8 1/2" 8 1/2" 9" 9"

Ruddy Turnstone
distinct black and white head and neck, rusty red back

non-breeding

Wilson's Snipe
striped head, long thick bill, bold stripes on back

Lesser Yellowlegs
long yellow legs, straight bill

Short-billed Dowitcher
rust and black back, long and slightly down-curved black bill

non-breeding

SANDPIPERS

9 1/2"

10"

10 1/2"

11"

Probing Feeders

Red Knot
rufous neck and chest, short dark bill, dark legs

non-breeding

American Woodcock
fat-bodied, dark cap, long thick bill

Long-billed Dowitcher
rufous barring, long and thick dark bill

non-breeding

Upland Sandpiper
long neck, small head, yellow bill

11"   11"   11 1/2"   12"

SANDPIPERS

Greater Yellowlegs
long yellow legs,
long upturned bill

Willet
long dark bill

non-breeding

Marbled Godwit
black legs, extremely
long upturned bill
with dark tip

non-breeding

Whimbrel
overall brown to gray, long
down-curved bill, dark stripe
through eyes

SANDPIPERS

14"   15"   18"   18"

Long-billed Curlew
gray legs, extremely long down-curved bill with dark tip

Piping Plover
thin black neck band, black forehead, black-tipped bill

non-breeding

Semipalmated Plover
wide black necklace, black across eyes, yellow legs

Wilson's Plover
single dark neck band and short, thick black bill

23"   7"   7"   7 1/2"

Killdeer
two black bands
around neck

non-breeding

American
Golden-Plover
black face to undertail,
white stripe on head
and neck

male

female

dark neck to belly, white
stripe on head and neck

Black-bellied Plover
black face to belly, white
cap, nape and undertail

non-breeding

PLOVERS

Wilson's Phalarope
large body, small
head, white throat

male

female

black stripe
down neck

PHALAROPE

11"

11"

11 1/2"

9 1/4"

Probing Feeders

Black-necked Stilt
black back, white belly,
ridiculously long orange legs

STILT

American Avocet
rusty head, upswept bill

non-breeding

American Oystercatcher
red-to-orange bill, black
"hood," yellow eyes with
orange eye-ring

AVOCET

Roseate Spoonbill
tall pink bird with
a distinctive, large
spoon-shaped bill

juvenile

IBIS

14" 18" 18 1/2" 32"

Cattle Egret
rusty-tinged head and back

Snowy Egret
black bill, yellow feet

Reddish Egret
slate-blue body, reddish neck
and head, bicolored bill

white morph

dark morph

Great Egret
yellow bill, black feet

EGRETS

20"

24"

30"

38"

Wading Feeders

Green Heron
rufous neck, orange legs and feet

Little Blue Heron
overall gray with greenish legs, bluish bill with dark tip

non-breeding

pure white with dark-tipped gray bill

juvenile

Yellow-crowned Night-Heron
bold white cheeks, red eyes

juvenile

light brown with dark bill, orange eyes

Black-crowned Night-Heron
black cap, large black bill

HERONS

19"

24"

24"

24 1/2"

HERONS

Tricolored Heron
white belly extending up the neck, bluish bicolored bill

Great Blue Heron
long neck, yellow bill

IBIS

Glossy Ibis
maroon with iridescent green-to-purple wings, dark eyes, long down-curved bill

non-breeding

White-faced Ibis
long down-curved gray bill, bright red legs

non-breeding

26"   47"   23"   23"

White Ibis
all white with long
down-curved orange
bill and orange legs

juvenile

IBIS

Wood Stork
all white with gray head,
long heavy bill, dark legs

STORK

25"

40"

Plunging Feeders

Least Tern
dark cap, white forehead, short yellow bill with black tip, dark wing tips

Black Tern
black head to belly, non-breeding white head to belly

Common Tern
black cap, thin red bill, non-breeding gray cap, black bill

Forster's Tern
black cap, orange base of bill, non-breeding lacks black cap

TERNS

9" 9 3/4" 14 1/2" 14 1/2"

Sandwich Tern
black cap, long dark bill with yellow tip, black legs

Black Skimmer
overall black with white face, distinctive large orange and black bill

Royal Tern
black cap, deep orange bill

Caspian Tern
black cap, large red bill, non-breeding partial black cap

TERNS

15"   18"   20"   21"

Bonaparte's Gull
black head, bill and wing tips, non-breeding ear patch on white head

Franklin's Gull
black head, dark red bill, non-breeding partial dark head, black bill

Laughing Gull
black "hood," dark orange bill, white crescents around eyes, black legs

Ring-billed Gull
black ring on bill, non-breeding speckled head

Lesser Black-backed Gull
dark gray to nearly black back and wings, yellow legs

13 1/2"   14 1/2"   16 1/2"   19"   23"

Scavenging Feeders

Herring Gull
yellow bill with orange dot, non-breeding speckled head

Glaucous Gull
light gray back and wings, heavy yellow bill, yellow eyes

Great Black-backed Gull
black back and wings, white head, large yellow bill with red spot

Magnificent Frigatebird
all black with angled, narrow wings and a long, forked tail

male

female

24 1/2"   27"   30"   40"

GULLS

FRIGATEBIRD

Dabbling Feeders

Sora
stout yellow bill, black mask

Purple Gallinule
red and yellow bill, yellow legs and feet

Common Gallinule
red forehead shield, yellow-tipped bill

American Coot
white bill

Limpkin
brown with white spots and long, slightly down-curved bill

American White Pelican
white with large yellow bill, black wing tips as seen in flight

RAILS

PELICAN

9"   13"   14"   14 1/2"   26"   62"

Double-crested Cormorant
long neck, yellow bill

Anhinga
long neck and tail, dagger-like pointed bill

male

female

Brown Pelican
white neck, dark brown pouch under long bill

33"   35"   48"

Adventure Quick Guides

Only Southeast and Gulf States Shorebirds

Organized by groups
for quick and easy identification

**Simple and convenient—narrow your choices
by group, and view just a few birds at a time**

- Pocket-sized format—easier than laminated foldouts

- Professional photos showing key markings

- Silhouettes and sizes for quick comparison

- Based on Stan Tekiela's best-selling bird field guides

Get these great *Adventure Quick Guides* for your area

ISBN 978-1-59193-656-5   **U.S. $9.95**

PUBLICATIONS
Adventure
an imprint of AdventureKEEN

NATURE/BIRDS/SOUTH